CYCLES IN SCIENCE

MATERIALS

PETER D. RILEY

Heinemann
LIBRARY

First published in Great Britain by Heinemann Library
Halley Court, Jordan Hill, Oxford OX2 8EJ
a division of Reed Educational and Professional Publishing Ltd.
Heinemann is a registered trademark of Reed Educational &
Professional Publishing Limited.

OXFORD FLORENCE PRAGUE MADRID ATHENS
MELBOURNE AUCKLAND KUALA LUMPUR SINGAPORE TOKYO
IBADAN NAIROBI KAMPALA JOHANNESBURG GABORONE
PORTSMOUTH NH CHICAGO MEXICO CITY SAO PAULO

Designed by Visual Image
Printed in Hong Kong

02 01 00 99
10 9 8 7 6 5 4 3 2 1

ISBN 0 431 08439 4
This title is also available in a hardback library edition (ISBN 0 431 08434 3).

British Library Cataloguing in Publication Data

Riley, Peter, 1947–
    Materials – (Cycles in science)
    1.Materials – Juvenile literature 2.Recycling (Waste, etc.)
    – Juvenile literature 3.Metamorphosis – Juvenile literature
    I.Title
    363.7'282

Acknowledgements

The Publishers would like to thank the following for
permission to reproduce photographs:
Bubbles: R Livermore p8; Bruce Coleman Ltd: A
Davies p26, C Lockwood p12, H Reinhard p21;
Michael Holford: p28; Planet Earth Pictures: B Brown
p15, A Jones p11, P Scoones p10; Science Photo
Library: D Guyon p20, R Maisonneuve p14, NASA
p29, D Parker p7, S Stammers p17; Tony Stone:
(Images) P Chesley p9, P Harris p16, R Magnusson
p6, J Willis p18, (Worldwide) S Jauncey p13, M
Leman p22; Trip: H Rogers p24; ZEFA: pp 4, 19,
Faltner p23, RGN p25, Ricatto p27, Rossenbach p5.

Cover photograph reproduced with permission of
Dr Jeremy Burgess, Science Photo Library

Our thanks to Jim Drake for his comments in the
preparation of this book.

Every effort has been made to contact copyright
holders of any material reproduced in this book. Any
omissions will be rectified in subsequent printings if
notice is given to the Publisher.

Any words appearing in the text in bold, **like
this**, are explained in the Glossary.

CONTENTS

MATERIALS

*Can you guess what is made of wood fibres, clay or chalk, wax and **pigments**? You are looking at it. It is this page. The wood fibres make up most of the paper. Particles of clay, or chalk, stick to the fibres and make the paper stronger and more **opaque**. The wax makes the paper more water-resistant and helps the ink stick to the paper. The pigments, which make the colours of the ink, come from oil. The oil is made from the bodies of ancient sea creatures that lived millions of years ago. Each one of the substances wood, clay, chalk, wax or pigment is a **material**. If this sheet of paper contains so many different materials from different places, imagine how many materials make up a car!*

PROPERTIES OF MATERIALS

A material has a range of useful **properties**. It may be hard and strong like steel or it may be soft and flexible. Many of the things we use, like this book, are made from more than one material. Each material is important because it has at least one useful property that the others do not. For example, the wood fibres in this page are not water resistant so they are coated with wax to prevent them falling apart if they get wet.

Cotton is a renewable material.

NATURAL AND MANUFACTURED

We use thousands of different materials. Some materials, like the wood fibres and the clay particles in this paper, are formed from natural materials. Other materials, like the pigments making these letters, are made by a series of processes which change one material into another. Materials which are changed greatly to make new materials are called raw materials. Oil, for example, is the raw material used for making pigments. The processes in which a raw material is used to make a new material are called the manufacturing processes and the new material is called a manufactured material.

Rock is a non-renewable material.

RENEWABLE AND NON-RENEWABLE

We never run out of some materials. They are produced by plants and animals every year. Two examples of these renewable materials are cotton and wool. Most materials are non-renewable. When they have been used up there is no more to replace them. Oil and metal ores are examples of non-renewable materials. As the human population grows, more and more materials are needed. We can save, or conserve, the stock of non-renewable materials on the planet by recycling materials we have already used.

WHAT ARE MATERIALS MADE FROM?

From early times people have wondered about materials and their properties. They formed ideas about them but most of these ideas were later shown to be wrong. One idea, about the elements, is still used today and has helped scientists understand the structure and the properties of materials. This information is still being used in developing new materials and recycling old ones.

ARE YOU MADE OF FIRE?

The first person in history to think about what things were made of was an ancient Greek **philosopher** called Thales. He believed that everything was made from the same basic substance, or element. He thought that as living things need water for life, then everything must be made of different forms of water. Other ancient Greek philosophers did not agree. Eventually it was decided that everything must be made from a mixture of four elements – water, air, fire and earth. This idea was used by scientists for more than 2000 years. You may still hear people today talk about the wind and rain as 'the elements'.

Many years ago, fire, water, air and earth were considered the four basic elements from which everything was made.

WHAT ARE THINGS REALLY MADE OF?

In 1661 an English scientist called Robert Boyle began testing the ancient Greeks' idea that materials were made from four elements. He discovered that air, water and earth could be broken down into simpler substances. We call these substances elements. For example, water is made from two elements called hydrogen and oxygen. So far, 109 elements have been discovered.

HOW SMALL CAN YOU GET?

What would happen if you took something and cut it in two, then took one half and cut that in two and so on? Eventually you would get to something so small that it could not be divided up any more. A Greek philosopher called Democritus had this idea over 2000 years ago. He called the smallest **particle** an atom, which is Greek for 'indivisible'. We still use his idea today although particles smaller than atoms have been discovered.

ELEMENTS, ATOMS AND RECYCLING

Scientists use their knowledge of how materials are made from elements, and how the atoms of elements join together, when they make new materials. They also use this knowledge to find new ways of recycling materials.

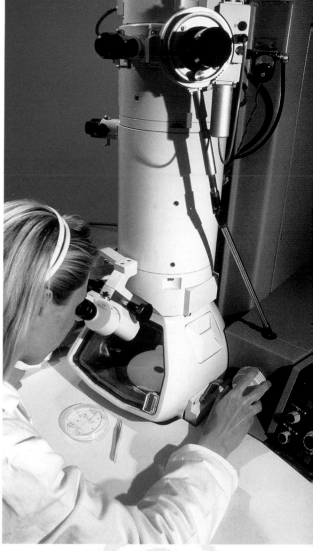

This **electron microscope** is being used to investigate the structure of materials. Some electron microscopes are so powerful that the arrangement of atoms within a material can be clearly seen.

THE STATES OF MATTER

Materials can exist in three ways. These are the three forms, or states, of matter. Materials change from one state to another when they reach a certain temperature. These temperature changes occur naturally. They can also be made to happen. Heat is used in manufacturing new materials or recycling old ones, so materials may change states during these processes too.

THREE STATES OF MATTER

Gas, liquid and solid are the three states of matter. The air is a mixture of gases and water is the most common liquid on this planet. Hailstones, which bounce off your head in a hailstorm, are solid while their temperature is low. But, when they warm up they melt into a liquid and then **evaporate** into a gas.

Carbon dioxide gas is squashed into drinks in cans and bottles.

What is your state of matter? Think of your bones, blood and lungs.

HOW CAN YOU TELL THEM APART?

A solid has a definite shape and **volume**. A liquid has no definite shape but it has a definite volume and it can be poured. A gas has no definite shape or volume. Unlike solids and liquids you can squash a gas and make it fill a smaller space. When you release it from a container, such as an aerosol spray can, it will spread out and fill any available space.

ALL CHANGE

All materials have melting points and boiling points. The melting point is the temperature at which a solid turns into a liquid. The boiling point is the temperature at which a liquid turns into a gas. Each substance has melting and boiling points that are different from other substances. The melting point of ice is 0 °C and the boiling point of water is 100 °C.

CHANGING STATES IN THE MATERIAL CYCLE

When iron ore is heated strongly with coke (made from coal) and limestone, the metal iron is released from the rock. This change takes place at such a high temperature that the metal is **molten**. It is poured into huge heat-resistant buckets to be taken away from the **furnace** to cool down and become solid again.

Glass that is collected from a recycling centre is mixed with raw materials for making new glass. The mixture is heated strongly so the raw materials can form new molten glass and the recycled glass also melts and mixes with it.

The molten rock flowing down the side of the **volcano** will cool and turn into a solid again.

9

THE WATER CYCLE

*Water is changed by four processes. They take place at normal temperatures on the Earth and allow water to exist in three forms on this planet. The processes are also a part of the water cycle which is the largest and fastest **material** cycle on the planet.*

THE CHANGING STATES OF WATER

Ice is solid water. When ice melts it becomes liquid water. Liquid water turns back into solid water by freezing at 0 °C. These processes are easy to see. The changes from liquid water to water **vapour** and back again are more difficult to observe.

Water changes from liquid into vapour by **evaporation**. In this process tiny **particles** of water escape from the liquid surface. Water vapour is a gas and mixes with the other gases in the air. Evaporation takes place faster in warmer conditions than in colder conditions.

The ice in this **glacier** is breaking up and toppling into the water. Eventually, the ice will melt into water, the next stage in the water cycle.

Water vapour changes back into liquid water by **condensation**. Droplets of water form on cool dust particles in the air and make a mist or cloud. They also form on cool surfaces. Your breath contains water vapour and when you breathe out onto a window pane the vapour condenses onto the cold glass.

Tiny particles of water escape from the lake's surface into the air. They form a vapour that usually cannot be seen. But in the cool air above this lake they have condensed to form tiny droplets which can be seen as a mist.

ROUND AND ROUND

A large amount of water evaporates from the surfaces of oceans, seas and lakes every day. It forms water vapour that rises into the air until it cools, condenses and forms water droplets that make clouds. When clouds reach cold regions over land they release their water as rain. This happens because the water droplets in the cloud freeze and form snowflakes. The snowflakes are too heavy to stay in the air so they fall through the clouds. As they fall they reach warmer air and melt, then they fall to the ground as drops of water. The rainwater forms streams and rivers which flow back to the oceans, seas and lakes where the water cycle can begin again.

WATER AND YOU

*Water is the main **material** in our bodies. Wherever people live there is a demand for clean water. Water is also used in food production and making other materials. Water is needed all the time so ways are being found to provide a constant supply from the water cycle.*

WATER AND YOU

You are awash with water. Nearly three-quarters of your weight is due to the amount of water in your body. You are thinking about this with a brain that is nearly four-fifths water and holding this book with bones that are much drier – less than a third of their weight is due to the water in them.

CLEANING UP WATER

Water rushing down a river carries twigs, grit, clay and **micro-organisms**. Before it can gush out of your tap, the water must be cleaned. First, the water passes through a metal grill which removes large objects like twigs and plastic bags.

These sprays are carefully positioned so the water reaches all the newly planted crops.

Second, chemicals called alum and lime are added. These stick to any clay and silt floating in the water and make them sink. Third, the water passes through a filter made of sand and gravel to trap any remaining **particles** in the water. Fourth, chlorine or ozone is bubbled through the water to kill the micro-organisms. Look at your next drink of water and think about what it has been through.

Waste water from a town goes to a sewage works where it is cleaned and released into a river.

USE OF WATER

Water is needed for growing crops and raising farm animals. Huge amounts of water are used to make all the different things around us. For example, it takes 8 litres of water to make a litre of lemonade and 30,000 litres of water to make all the items in a car – from its steel body to its rubber tyres.

SUPPLYING DEMAND

The amount of water in a river varies through the year as the weather changes between dry and wet weather. A river cannot supply a constant amount of water so a **dam** might be built across it to flood a valley and make a reservoir. Some places do not receive enough rainfall. Water is transported to these places along underground pipes from distant reservoirs.

This dam has trapped the river water behind it to fill the valley and give a constant supply of water.

LIVING THINGS

Plants and animals provide us with renewable materials. The materials they make as they grow are essential in their lives but humans can make use of these materials too.

THE CYCLE OF LIFE

This material, which looks like snow, is wood **pulp** that is about to be flattened into sheets of paper. A sample is being taken to check the wood pulp process is working correctly.

Plants make food using the energy from sunlight, carbon dioxide from the air and water and **minerals** from the soil. They use the food to grow and to reproduce. Animals eat the plants and use the food for growth and reproduction too. When plants and animals die their bodies rot away and form carbon dioxide in the air and minerals in the soil. They are recycled with water and more sunlight into more living things. The materials we use from living things such as wood, **fibres** and leather are renewable as they are part of the life cycle of plants or animals.

WOOD

Wood is a strong material made by trees to hold up leaves to the sunlight. It is made from tiny pipes and fibres which are arranged in rings inside the trunk and branches. The shape and thickness of the fibres give the wood its **properties**. The wood may be light in weight and easily cut like the balsa wood used in model aeroplanes or it may be hard and tough like the wood in a ball used in a game of bowls.

Paper is made by separating the fibres in the wood and making them into a pulp.

COTTON

Cotton plants make seeds covered in fibres (see picture on page 4). The fibres are removed and twisted into threads called cotton yarn. This is woven into cotton shirts, denim jeans and other clothes.

These sheep are being shorn. Their thick, woolly coats will be used to make wool for clothing.

WOOL

Wool is made from fibres which grow out of a sheep's skin. The wavy fibres are covered in scales and under the microscope look a little like crocodile tails. The wavy, scaly structure of the fibres stops them packing too closely together and allows air to get trapped between them. The air stops heat quickly passing out of the sheep's body and keeps it warm. This makes wool a good heat insulator and woollen yarn is used in clothes to keep you warm.

LEATHER

Leather is made from the skins of cattle which are called hides. Inside the skin is a network of fibres which make the skin strong and flexible. After processing the hide, the fibres still remain to make a strong flexible material for shoes and boots.

ROCKS

The cycle of rocks through the environment is very slow. Rocks may come from below the Earth's surface or they may form on the surface or in the sea. Rocks are made from crystals of minerals which may change if the rocks are heated.

The pebbles in this stream bed have come from the rocks in the mountains beyond the bridge.

THE ROCK CYCLE

The Earth has a rocky **crust**. Underneath is a hot, semi-liquid rocky interior. The heat melts the rock in the lower part of the crust. The **molten** rock moves upwards. It may become trapped in the crust and cool down slowly to form **granite** or it may escape through the mouth of a **volcano** and cool down quickly to form **basalt**. Rocks which form in this way are called igneous rocks (see picture on page 9).

Rock is affected by the weather. When water gets into cracks and freezes, the ice that forms pushes the rock apart and breaks it into pieces. These are carried by rivers. The smallest **particles** eventually settle down and form a layer of sand. In time, the layer gets so thick and heavy that the particles are squashed together and form **sandstone**. These rocks are called sedimentary rocks.

The Earth's crust is divided into huge slabs called **plates**. The movement of the semi-liquid rock beneath them pushes some of them together. Where this happens one plate is forced under the other. The rocks in the sinking plate get hot and the cycle can begin again. The rock cycle takes hundreds of millions of years.

ROCKS FROM SHELLS

Many sea creatures make shells for protection. They use chemicals dissolved in the sea water to make their shells. When the creatures die their shells sink to the sea bed and form a layer. In time, as more die, the layer gets thicker and heavier and turns into rock. Limestone and chalk are both formed in this way.

The fossil of the hard body of this ancient sea creature can be seen on the surface of this piece of limestone.

ROCKS AND MINERALS

Rocks are made from crystals that interlock and make them strong. The crystals are made from minerals. A mineral is a substance that is made from one or more elements. For example, a common mineral found in many kinds of rock is silica. It is made from the elements called silicon and oxygen.

CHANGING FORMS

Some of the rocks in the Earth's crust are squashed together as the plates move. They form new mountain ranges. The pressure, due to squashing, heats the rocks strongly over a long time. The rock crystals melt and reform in a different way. The changed rock is called metamorphic rock.

ROCKY MATERIALS

*Rocks have **properties** that make them particularly useful for building. Clay is formed from rocks and is used in building and making pottery. Limestone is used in making cement and forms part of a mixture with sand to make glass – a rocky material that humans can help recycle.*

USING ROCKS

Igneous rocks like **granite** and **basalt** are very hard and are used for making concrete. The **mineral crystals** in granite are large and make the rock look attractive when its surface is polished. Polished granite blocks are used as decoration for the front of important buildings like museums and banks. They form part of the supporting structure too.

Sedimentary rocks form thick hard layers or beds. Between the layers are boundaries called bedding planes where the rocks are easier to cut. **Sandstone** and limestone are used as building stone because they are strong but easy to cut into small sizes.

Marble and slate are metamorphic rocks. Marble is a strong rock with an attractive surface and is used for decoration. Slate splits into thin waterproof sheets and is used as a roofing material.

CLAY

Clay is made from very small **particles** that form when rocks like granite are **weathered**. Different types of clay are used for making bricks and pottery.

When clay is mixed with water it is easy to mould and shape.

The clay is mixed with water and shaped into a brick or a cup. Then it is heated strongly in a **furnace** called a kiln. The heat makes the tiny particles stick together where they touch and form a rigid structure which is strong but brittle.

CEMENT AND CONCRETE

Cement is made by heating limestone and clay together. It is used to join bricks in a wall or gravel in concrete. When water is added to cement it forms interlocking crystals that bind bricks together or make concrete set hard.

GLASS

Sand, limestone and a chemical called soda are heated together to make glass. Glass is a hard, strong, transparent substance which cleans easily and does not rot. Sheets of glass are used in windows because they let in light but keep out wind and rain without weathering like rock.

RECYCLING ROCKY MATERIALS

When old stone buildings are pulled down, the stones may be used to build something else or they may be crushed and used in the foundations of roads. Clay cannot be recycled but glass can. Recycling glass saves sand, limestone and soda. Less energy is used to recycle glass than to make it from raw **materials**, so fuels are saved too.

This **molten** glass is so weak it can be blown into a ball. Only ornamental glassware is made in this way.

19

METALS

*Metals have many useful **properties** and are used to make a wide range of things. Very few metals are found in their pure metallic state. Most metals are found in rocks called ores. Energy is needed to release the metal from the ore once it has been mined. Large amounts of iron and aluminium are recycled.*

Red hot steel from a **furnace** is being rolled into a thin sheet.

PROPERTIES AND USES OF METALS

Metals are strong shiny **materials** that can be shaped or pulled into long thin wires. They are good **conductors** of electricity and heat. These properties have been used in a variety of ways to make a huge range of items. Cars and lorries, wristwatches, cutlery, pans, zips, coins and the wire in a light bulb are all made of metals.

THE AGES OF METAL

Most metals are naturally combined with other substances in rocks called ores. Nearly 4000 years ago, tin was discovered by heating rocks. It was mixed with copper, which is found naturally, to make a stronger metal called bronze. The period of time when most metal objects were made of bronze is called the Bronze Age.

About 2500 years ago people learnt how to increase the heat in a fire with **bellows** and discovered that certain rocks would release iron. Iron is stronger than bronze so metal workers changed over to using it. This was the beginning of the Iron Age. Iron is still the main metal we use today. Much of it is changed into steel.

ALUMINIUM – THE LATE ARRIVAL

Aluminium is the most common metal on the Earth but huge amounts of energy are needed to release it from its ore. In 1886 two chemists, Charles Hall and Paul Heroult, discovered a way of extracting aluminium easily by using electricity. Today the strong, lightweight properties of aluminium are used to make bodies for aircraft and coaches, and the cables for overhead power lines. Aluminium is not poisonous and does not contaminate food, so it is used to make drink cans and thin sheets of it are used for wrapping all kinds of food to keep them fresh.

RECYCLING METALS

Up to half of the iron and aluminium in use today will be recycled. This will save some of the non-renewable ores and fuel and energy needed to **extract** the metals.

The steel in these old car bodies will be taken back to the steelworks and mixed with new iron to make more steel. The recycled metal may be turned into another car.

PLASTIC

*Oil and gas are the raw **materials** used for making plastic. Oil is a mixture of many substances which can be separated by **evaporation** and **condensation**. There are two major kinds of plastic but they are not easy to recycle.*

IN TOUCH WITH THE PAST

Next time you pick up a plastic pen remind yourself that you are holding a material which comes from a substance that formed 200 million years ago. It came from the bodies of tiny plants and animals that lived in the sea. When they died they sank to the sea floor where **micro-organisms** got to work on **decomposing** their bodies. The micro-organisms used oxygen in the water as they fed but they ran out of oxygen before everything had decomposed. The remains formed a thick layer that was buried by sand. In time the sand turned to rock and the remains turned to gas and oil. Today the rocks are drilled to release the gas and oil.

An oil refinery where the hydrocarbons in oil are separated and prepared for making a range of products.

BOILING OIL

Oil is a mixture of substances called **hydrocarbons**. Each one has a different boiling point from the others. They are separated by running hot oil into the bottom of a tall tower. Most of the hydrocarbons evaporate and rise up the tower.

The hydrocarbon **vapour** gets cooler and cooler as it rises and only those hydrocarbons with the lowest boiling points reach the top and are stored as gases. The other hydrocarbons condense at different levels in the tower and are collected separately. The hydrocarbons which condense near the top of the tower are used to make plastics.

Plastics are made into thousands of different products from gloves and brushes to containers of almost any shape.

HARD AND SOFT

There are two kinds of plastic. Thermoplastics are plastics that become soft and melt when they are warmed (like polystyrene cups or perspex sheets). Thermosetting plastics do not melt when heated. They are used for making plastic cases, kitchen working surfaces and table tops. Bakelite ®, melamine and Formica ® are examples of thermosetting plastics.

RECYCLING PLASTIC

Few plastics are easy to recycle. One plastic that can be recycled is called PET, which stands for polythene terephthalate. It is used to make plastic bottles. After the bottles have been collected for recycling they are cleaned, broken down into small pieces and melted to make the plastic ready for shaping and using again.

ROTTING AWAY

*You are made up of chemicals which are constantly being recycled. The chemicals in **materials** made by other living things also recycle quickly and can be put to good use. But the chemicals in some materials may stay where they are for ever.*

THE CHEMICAL ROUNDABOUT

You contain more chemicals than a chemistry set. They originally come from water, the air and **minerals** in the soil. Plants make them into food. When you eat a meal your body uses most of them to stay alive and grow. You get rid of the chemicals you do not need as wastes. **Micro-organisms** break down wastes into chemicals which pass back into the air and the soil. When any other living thing dies the micro-organisms break that down too. This recycling of chemicals has been taking place on the Earth for over 3000 million years. Some chemicals in you today may have been in a lettuce last week, and in a 100 years time they may be in a tree.

These potato plants have used the minerals in the compost to make this crop.

WHAT WILL ROT?

A substance such as wood, wool or cotton, which can break down completely to simple chemicals, and which can be used again by living things, is called a **biodegradable** substance. Kitchen wastes such as potato peelings and carrot tops are biodegradable. Iron and steel are not biodegradable because they break down to rust which cannot be used by living things. Nothing rots aluminium or glass.

Almost all plastics are not biodegradable but a biodegradable plastic made from sugar has recently been invented. When you throw it away, micro-organisms break it down into carbon dioxide and water.

USING WASTES

Many gardeners collect up dead plants and micro-organisms rot them down into a substance called compost. Gardeners dig the compost back into the soil. It provides **minerals** for another crop of vegetables or a display of flowers.

In some parts of the world wastes from humans, animals and the kitchen are used to make methane gas, which can be used as a fuel to cook meals. The wastes are stored in pits to rot. As the micro-organisms feed on the wastes they make methane gas. It rises to the top of the pit and is drawn off along a pipe connected to a kitchen stove.

At a rubbish tip materials that will rot are stored with materials that will not rot but could be recycled. Both are being stored uselessly.

HOW RECYCLING HELPS

There is only a certain amount of each type of raw material on Earth. Most raw materials are underground and covered by habitats such as woodlands and rainforests. Energy is needed to manufacture materials and this comes from fuel which is also underground. When materials are thrown away they create environmental problems. Everyone throws away a large amount of rubbish. Recycling could help us and our planet Earth.

SAVING RAW MATERIALS

These items are being sorted at a recycling centre. They will be taken away to be made into new products. Some of the new products may find their way back here.

Each day the amount of raw materials on Earth gets smaller. They are being used up to make the new things we need for our modern way of life. As a raw material becomes scarce it becomes more difficult and more expensive to **extract**. Recycling reduces the amount of a raw material that needs to be extracted. This means it will last longer and will remain cheaper for longer.

SAVING ENERGY

Energy is needed to extract the raw materials and process them to make metals, glass and plastic. Most of the energy comes from fuels which are non-renewable. Recycling material saves fuel because less raw material has to be extracted and processed.

SAVING HABITATS

When raw materials and fuels like coal are extracted, the land above them may be cleared of trees and plants. This allows digging machines to reach them and also makes it easy for trucks to take them away. The habitats of plants and animals are destroyed when land is cleared. Recycling material also saves habitats because there is less need for raw materials and fuel.

RECYCLING AND RUBBISH

In the past, rubbish has been stored in tips made from disused quarries. As the tips become full new places for waste are needed. Recycling reduces the demand for tipping space and prevents more habitats from being destroyed.

A large area of natural habitat has been cleared away to make room for diggers to extract the copper ore in this open-cast mine.

A PILE OF RUBBISH

Every year the people living in your home may produce a tonne of rubbish. If everyone at your school came from a home that produced the same amount of rubbish how many tonnes would the rubbish pile weigh? Imagine that pile of rubbish being produced by the families of everyone in your school every year. Think of the materials that could be recycled and the habitats that could be saved.

THE FUTURE

*Our supplies of raw **materials** will not last for ever but we can make replacements. Recycling now will help prepare for the future. In time our search for new materials may take us beyond the Earth.*

WHAT IS LEFT?

The Earth has been searched for all traces of non-renewable materials. The amounts of each one have been calculated. These amounts are based on how long a raw material would last if we used it up as we do now. For example, the amount of aluminium ore left to be mined from places we can easily reach will last for over 200 years. If the ore in places that are difficult to reach is included we have enough aluminium left to last us nearly 800 years. Most other raw materials will not last that long.

USING OUR BRAINS

Humans have existed on this planet for about 2 million years. At first they only used natural materials like stone and renewable ones like wood. It was 8000 years ago that people discovered how to **extract** metal from their ores and in the last 100 years plastics have been developed and widely used. Today there are thousands of materials that have been discovered or invented.

The materials and technology used in the flint axes of the Stone Age.

In the future more work will be done to discover ways of using renewable materials instead of non-renewable ones. Plastics are made from oil now, but in future they may be made from plants.

Although we will eventually run out of the non-renewable materials, we have the intelligence and knowledge of materials to help us replace them.

RECYCLING GIVES US TIME

The human population is expected to reach 10 billion by the end of the 21st century so the demand for materials will continue to increase. Recycling the materials we use today will save more raw materials and fuel for the future and give us longer to prepare for the time when they are used up.

FUTURE AND PAST

The **properties** of stone allowed us to chop wood and the properties of wood allowed us to build homes. Today, the properties of materials we have discovered or invented have allowed us to begin exploring space. In the future we may be able to use raw materials from the Moon or asteroids. By then, people may look back at the materials we use today and think of them as we think of the rocks and pebbles used by our ancestors in the Stone Age. Whatever happens, the material cycle will continue to turn.

The materials in these spacesuits keep the astronauts safe as they repair a satellite brought on board the Space Shuttle.

GLOSSARY

basalt an igneous rock (formed from molten rock beneath the Earth's crust) which cooled quickly and has fine grains

bellows a machine which is used to suck in air and blow it out to increase the temperature of a fire by increasing the speed of burning

biodegradable a property of a material which allows it to be broken down by micro-organisms into simple substances such as water and carbon dioxide

condensation changing from a gas or a vapour into a liquid

conductor a material through which heat or electricity can pass easily

crust the rocky layer which covers the surface of the Earth both on land and beneath the sea

crystal a piece of solid which has flat sides arranged in an orderly way

dam a structure built across a river to prevent the flow of water and to store it in a reservoir

decompose to break down into tiny particles and simple substances

electron microscope a very high powered microscope which uses electrons instead of light to investigate the structure of materials

element a substance which cannot be broken down into simpler substances and is made of only one kind of atom

evaporation changing from a liquid into a gas or a vapour

extract to take out

fibre a very small piece of solid which is long, thin and flexible

furnace a structure in which a large amount of heat can be generated

glacier a huge ice structure made by compacted snow which flows overland and breaks up to form a river or enters the sea

granite an igneous rock (formed from molten rock beneath the Earth's crust) which cooled slowly and has large grains

hydrocarbon a chemical substance made from the two elements hydrogen and oxygen

material a substance which is a solid, liquid or gas

micro-organism a tiny living thing, such as bacteria; it can only be seen with the use of a microscope

mineral a substance in the soil needed by living things or a rocky substance which contains useful materials such as metal

molten the liquid state into which a solid changes when it melts

opaque does not let light pass through

particle a very small piece of a substance

philosopher a person who uses observations and reason to try to understand and explain how things are formed and how they work

pigment small particles, such as those in a powder, that are used to colour an object when made into a paint or ink

plate a large slab of the Earth's rocky crust which moves slowly over the surface of the planet's hot interior

preservative a substance which will stop the decomposition of a material

property a special feature of a material such as its shiny surface or its ability to conduct electricity

pulp mashed up fibres mixed with water

sandstone a rock made by sand grains that have been squashed close together

vapour a kind of gas which easily escapes from the surface of a liquid but condenses back to a liquid when it is cooled

volcano an opening in the Earth's crust through which molten rock, ash and gases come out

volume the amount of space occupied by a substance

weathered where rocks have broken down due to changes in temperature, water and wind

INDEX